Author's Note

This book features 100 influential and inspiring quotes by Buddha. Undoubtedly, this collection will give you a huge boost of inspiration. It's amazing that his wisdom still resonates in today's life.

D1106213

1

"If you knew what I know about the power of giving you would not let a single meal pass without sharing it in some way."

2

"Give, even if you only have a little."

3

"Those who cling to perceptions and views wander the world offending people."

4

"I never see what has been done;
I only see what remains to be
done."

5

"You only lose what you cling to."

6

"The past is already gone, the future is not yet here. There's only one moment for you to live."

7

"The trouble is, you think you
have time."

8

"Your work is to discover your work and then with all your heart to give yourself to it."

9

"Believe nothing, no matter where you read it, or who said it, no matter if I have said it, unless it agrees with your own reason and your own common sense."

10

"The tongue like a sharp knife...
Kills without drawing blood."

11

"Teach this triple truth to all: A generous heart, kind speech, and a life of service and compassion are the things which renew humanity."

12

"Drop by drop is the water pot filled. Likewise, the wise man, gathering it little by little, fills himself with good."

13

"I will not look at another's bowl intent on finding fault: a training to be observed."

14

"Let none find fault with others; let none see the omissions and commissions of others. But let one see one's own acts, done and undone."

15

"Should a person do good, let him do it again and again. Let him find pleasure therein, for blissful is the accumulation of good."

16

"May all beings have happy minds."

17

"Delight in heedfulness! Guard well your thoughts!"

18

"To abstain from lying is essentially wholesome."

19

"Holding onto anger is like drinking poison and expecting the other person to die."

20

"Should you find a wise critic to point out your faults, follow him as you would a guide to hidden treasure."

21

"Should a seeker not find a companion who is better or equal, let them resolutely pursue a solitary course."

22

"Hatred is never appeased by hatred in this world. By non-hatred alone is hatred appeased. This is a law eternal."

23

"Live with no sense of 'mine,' not forming attachment to experiences."

24

"Better it is to live one day seeing the rise and fall of things than to live a hundred years without ever seeing the rise and fall of things."

25

"One is not called noble who harms living beings. By not harming living beings one is called noble."

26

"If a man going down into a river, swollen and swiftly flowing, is carried away by the current — how can he help others across?"

27

"We are born of love; Love is our mother."

28

"All conditioned things are impermanent—when one sees this with wisdom, one turns away from suffering."

29

"Ardently do today what must be done. Who knows? Tomorrow, death comes."

30

"The world is afflicted by death and decay. But the wise do not grieve, having realized the nature of the world."

31

"Resolutely train yourself to attain peace."

32

"To support mother and father, to cherish wife and children, and to be engaged in peaceful occupation — this is the greatest blessing."

33

"What you think, you become.
What you feel, you attract.
What you imagine, you create."

34

"All tremble at violence; all fear death. Putting oneself in the place of another, one should not kill nor cause another to kill."

35

"They blame those who remain silent, they blame those who speak much, they blame those who speak in moderation. There is none in the world who is not blamed."

36

"Just as the great ocean has one taste, the taste of salt, so also this teaching and discipline has one taste, the taste of liberation."

37

"If with a pure mind a person speaks or acts, happiness follows them like a never-departing shadow."

38

"As an elephant in the battlefield withstands arrows shot from bows all around, even so shall I endure abuse."

39

"The one in whom no longer exist the craving and thirst that perpetuate becoming; how could you track that Awakened one, trackless, and of limitless range."

40

"There are only two mistakes one can make along the road to truth; not going all the way, and not starting."

41

"No one saves us but ourselves. No one can and no one may. We ourselves must walk the path."

42

"If a man's thoughts are muddy,
If he is reckless and full of
deceit, How can he wear the
yellow robe? Whoever is master
of his own nature, Bright, clear
and true, He may indeed wear
the yellow robe."

43

"The root of suffering is attachment."

44

"Whatever precious jewel there is in the heavenly worlds, there is nothing comparable to one who is Awakened."

45

"As a water bead on a lotus leaf, as water on a red lily, does not adhere, so the sage does not adhere to the seen, the heard, or the sensed."

46

"It is in the nature of things that joy arises in a person free from remorse."

47

"All experiences are preceded by mind, having mind as their master, created by mind."

48

"Purity and impurity depend on oneself; no one can purify another."

49

"Ceasing to do evil, Cultivating the good, Purifying the heart: This is the teaching of the Buddhas."

50

"Understanding is the heartwood of well-spoken words."

51

"He who can curb his wrath as soon as it arises, as a timely antidote will check snake's venom that so quickly spreads — such a monk gives up the here and the beyond, just as a serpent sheds its worn-out skin."

52

"As I am, so are these. As are these, so am I. Drawing the parallel to yourself, neither kill nor get others to kill."

53

"Anger will never disappear so long as thoughts of resentment are cherished in the mind. Anger will disappear just as soon as thoughts of resentment are forgotten."

54

"If you are quiet enough, you will hear the flow of the universe. You will feel its rhythm. Go with this flow. Happiness lies ahead. Meditation is key."

55

"Just as a solid rock is not shaken by the storm, even so the wise are not affected by praise or blame."

56

"We will develop love, we will practice it, we will make it both a way and a basis..."

57

"There is no fear for one whose mind is not filled with desires."

58

"Whatever is not yours: let go of it. Your letting go of it will be for your long-term happiness & benefit."

59

"The one in whom no longer exist the craving and thirst that perpetuate becoming; how could you track that Awakened one, trackless, and of limitless range?"

60

"Peace comes from within. Do not seek it without."

61

"Those who are free of resentful thoughts surely find peace."

62

"There has to be evil so that good can prove its purity above it."

63

"To conquer oneself is a greater task than conquering others."

64

"The whole secret of existence is to have no fear. Never fear what will become of you, depend on no one. Only the moment you reject all help are you freed."

65

"Meditate ... do not delay, lest you later regret it."

66

"Whatever has the nature of arising has the nature of ceasing."

67

"Resolutely train yourself to attain peace."

68

"Know from the rivers in clefts and in crevices: those in small channels flow noisily, the great flow silent. Whatever's not full makes noise. Whatever is full is quiet."

69

"Whatever living beings there may be — feeble or strong, long, stout, or of medium size, short, small, large, those seen or those unseen, those dwelling far or near, those who are born as well as those yet to be born — may all beings have happy minds."

70

"If you knew what I know about the power of giving, you would not let a single meal pass without sharing it in some way."

71

"Let him not deceive another nor despise anyone anywhere. In anger or ill will let him not wish another ill."

72

"Our life is shaped by our mind; we become what we think. Suffering follows an evil thought as the wheels of a cart follow the oxen that draw it. Our life is shaped by our mind; we become what we think. Joy follow a pure thought like a shadow that never leaves."

73

"If you meditate earnestly, pure in mind and kind in deeds, leading a disciplined life in harmony with the dharma, you will grow in glory. If you meditate earnestly, through spiritual disciplines you can make an island for yourself that no flood can overwhelm."

74

"Good people keep on walking whatever happens. They do not speak vain words and are the same in good fortune and bad. If one desires neither children nor wealth nor power nor success by unfair means, know such a one to be good, wise, and virtuous."

75

"One who conquers himself is greater than another who conquers a thousand times a thousand men on the battlefield. Be victorious over yourself and not over others."

76

"Everything that has a beginning has an ending. Make your peace with that and all will be well."

77

"Yesterday I was clever, so I wanted to change the world. Today I am wise, so I am changing myself."

78

"The only real failure in life is not to be true to the best one knows."

79

"However many holy words you read, However many you speak, What good will they do you If you do not act on upon them?"

80

"If we could see the miracle of a single flower clearly, our whole life would change."

81

"Those who have failed to work toward the truth have missed the purpose of living."

82

"In separateness lies the world's greatest misery; in compassion lies the world's true strength."

83

"Your own self is your master; who else could be? With yourself well controlled, you gain a master very hard to find."

84

"Not by rituals and resolutions, nor by much learning, nor by celibacy, nor even by meditation can you find the supreme, immortal joy of nirvana until you extinguish your self-will."

"It seems that although we thought ourselves permanent, we are not. Although we thought ourselves settled, we are not. Although we thought we would last forever, we will not."

86

"If you do not change direction, you may end up where you are heading."

87

"Health is the best gift, contentment the best wealth, trust the best kinsman, nirvana the greatest joy. Drink the nectar of the dharma in the depths of meditation, and become free from fear and sin."

88

"Nothing can harm you as much
as your own thoughts
unguarded."

"One moment can change a day, one day can change a life, and one life can change the world.

"Faith and prayer both are invisible, but they make impossible things possible."

91

"If you find no one to support you on the spiritual path, walk alone. There is no companionship with the immature."

92

"Work out your own salvation.
Do not depend on others."

93

"All wrong-doing arises because of mind. If mind is transformed can wrong-doing remain?"

94

"It is a man's own mind, not his enemy or foe, that lures him to evil ways."

95

"There is nothing so disobedient as an undisciplined mind, and there is nothing so obedient as a disciplined mind."

96

"You will not be punished for your anger, you will be punished by your anger."

97

"If the problem can be solved why worry? If the problem cannot be solved worrying will do you no good."

98

"Chaos is inherent in all compounded things. Strive on with diligence."

99

"Everything that happens to us is the result of what we ourselves have thought, said, or done. We alone are responsible for our lives."

100

"Even as a solid rock is unshaken by the wind, so are the wise unshaken by praise or blame."

Made in the USA
Middletown, DE
05 November 2023

41980255R00056